MAKE it WORK!

SPACE

Andrew Haslam

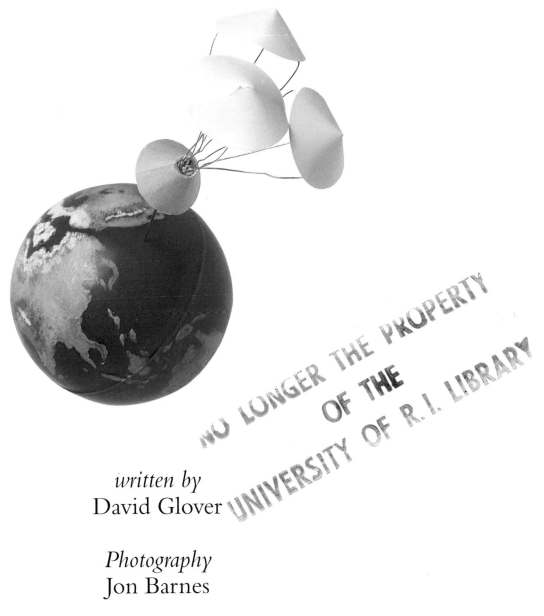

written by
David Glover

Photography
Jon Barnes

Action Publishing

Make it Work!
Other titles

Body
Building
Earth
Electricity
Flight
Insects
Machines
Photography
Plants
Sound
Time

Action Publishing
A Division of Action Products International, Inc.
344 Cypress Road
Ocala, FL 34472-3108

First published in Great Britain by
Two-Can Publishing Ltd.

Printed in Hong Kong

ISBN: 1-882210-49-2

Editor: Christine Morley
Series Editor: Kate Asser
Assistant Editors: Jacqueline McCann, Robert Sved
Series concept and design: Andrew Haslam and Wendy Baker
Additional design: Paul Miller

Thanks to everyone at Plough Studios

Contents

Words marked in **bold** in the text are explained in the glossary.

You can do many exciting things as an astronomer: study the sun and moon, plan rocket expeditions to explore the planets, search for **black holes**, and come up with theories about how the universe began and how it might end.

MAKE it WORK!

You don't need expensive or complicated equipment to be an astronomer. With just a warm coat and a star chart, you can go outside on a clear night and start to learn the names of the stars. Building the models in this book will show you the differences between the planets, stars, and **galaxies** that you spot and help you to understand how the universe works.

Now is a very exciting time in the history of astronomy. Powerful telescopes, modern computers, and sophisticated **space probes** help astronomers to see farther and more clearly into space than ever before.

You will need

You can build most of the models out of cheap, easily available materials, such as cardboard, wood, marbles, plastic containers, and other odds and ends. You will need some tools to cut the materials; all of the equipment above will be very useful as part of your astronomer's kit.

Using lights

Some of the projects use light bulbs powered by batteries. Flashlights are also used, and the bulbs in these and the battery-operated bulbs are safe to handle. However, if you use a low-voltage lamp, always ask an adult to set it up for you.

Warning! Never look at the sun through binoculars or a telescope.

You will need some simple tools to plan projects and to record observations. Star charts, which you can find in astronomy books or buy separately, are a handy way to find your way around the night sky. Binoculars, **lenses**, and a **magnetic compass** will all be useful.

Safety!

Sharp tools are dangerous! Take care when you use them and ask an adult to help you. Make sure that anything you are cutting or drilling is held firmly so that it cannot slip. A small table vise is ideal for holding pieces of wood.

Ancient peoples believed that Earth was the center of the universe. Their belief was based on what they could feel and see – Earth under our feet feels as if it is still, and it looks as though the sun, the moon, and the stars move around Earth. But now we know that it is really Earth that moves around the sun. The sun only appears to be moving through the sky because Earth spins on its **axis** as it travels through space.

MAKE it WORK!
This model of the sun, Earth, and moon shows how Earth's spin gives us day and night.

You will need
tape
plasticine
a bradawl
a protractor
a small rubber ball
two pieces of wire
a paintbrush and paints
a large sponge rubber ball
a light bulb in a holder or
   a bright flashlight
a wooden or plastic bead

1 The large sponge rubber ball is Earth. Paint a map of the world on it, using green, yellow, and blue paint. Use white to show the ice at the poles.

2 Ask an adult to help you make a hole through Earth, from pole to pole, with the bradawl.

3 Push Earth onto the straight wire and slip the bead onto the foot of the wire. Fix the wire to a flat base with a blob of plasticine.

4 The light bulb is the sun. Earth **orbits** the sun, spinning on its axis (the wire in the model) as it moves. The axis is tilted to the orbit by 23°. Show this in your model by fixing the wire to the protractor at 67° from the horizontal.

5 Add the small ball to your model by fixing it on a bent wire, as shown. This is the moon. Push the wire into the hole in the bead, and secure both wires with tape. The moon orbits Earth.

*The sun is our nearest star. It is a huge ball of flame, 93 million miles away, that warms Earth. The sun's power comes from a **nuclear reaction** called fusion. Without the warmth of the sun, Earth would be a cold, lifeless ball of rock.*

Earth is a planet in orbit around the sun. It is about 8,000 miles in diameter and is the only planet in the solar system with liquid water on its surface. At the North and South poles, which get very little sunlight, the water has frozen into ice caps.

On the side of Earth facing the sun it is daytime. The side facing away from the sun is in the dark shadow of night. Earth spins on its axis, completing a rotation once every 24 hours. Try turning your Earth model to see how different places on Earth move from day to night.

Looking down on the North Pole, Earth spins counterclockwise. This means that we are moving from west to east. As we move from the night shadow into daylight, the sun seems to rise in the east. At the end of the day, the sun appears to set in the west.

We use the motion of Earth to measure time. It takes a day (24 hours) for Earth to spin once on its axis, and 365¼ days for Earth to orbit the sun. Shadows cast by objects blocking the sun's light move as Earth spins. You can chart the shadows throughout the day with a sundial and use it to tell the time.

You will need

glue	tape
scissors	a watch
a craft knife	a stencil
thin and thick cardboard	a rubber band
a small magnetic compass with a moving scale	

1 For the sundial base, cut two rectangles of thick cardboard, 6 in. x 3 in. Then cut out two rectangles of thin cardboard to the same dimensions and glue on top of thick cardboard. Join rectangles together on one side only with tape.

gnomon

MAKE it WORK!

Sundials were probably the first clocks. You can make a simple sundial by sticking a pole in the ground and marking the position of the shadow with stones at different times of the day. The portable sundial, above, has a compass, so that you can line it up with north each time you use it.

2 Cut out a third rectangle of thin cardboard, 12 in. x 3 in. Ask an adult to help you cut a slit in the center. Glue cardboard to base rectangle.

3 Cut sundial face and three legs, one of which includes dial pointer, or **gnomon**, from thin cardboard, as shown left. The gnomon is 3 in. long.

4 Ask an adult to help you cut a slot in the dial face for the gnomon. Fold and glue the leg flaps to assemble the sundial, as shown below. Glue the gnomon foot into the central slit.

5 Glue the compass to one end of the base. With an adult's help, cut a hole in the other end, so that the compass will rest in it when folded. Keep the sundial closed with a rubber band.

7 Now you must find north on the sundial. If you live in the Northern **Hemisphere** (for example, in the United States or Europe), then you must line up the sundial so that the straight edge of the pointer faces south. But if you live in the Southern Hemisphere (for example, in Australia or New Zealand) then the pointer should face north.

8 Look at the compass and mark north on the base, as shown. If you are in the Northern Hemisphere, turn the sundial until the compass points south. If you are in the Southern Hemisphere, point the compass north. Look at your watch and, without moving the dial, mark the position of the gnomon's shadow every hour.

Calibrating your sundial

6 Now that your sundial is complete, you are ready to **calibrate** it. This means making marks to scale, at certain points on the dial, so that you can read the time from it in the future. You will need to do this on a sunny day. Stand your sundial on a flat surface in the sun, so that you can see a shadow cast by the pointer on the face of the dial.

9 Slide the gnomon out of the dial and number the marks, using a stencil. Carefully slide the gnomon back into position.

When you have calibrated your sundial you can tell the time just by lining up the compass and looking at the position of the shadow. Now you will only need to use your watch at night!

If you live north of the **equator**, the month of December falls in the middle of winter. But if you live south of the equator, it is in the middle of summer.

MAKE it WORK!

Building this model will help you see why the seasons – spring, summer, autumn, and winter – happen at different times north and south of the equator.

You will need

a protractor	glue
a large bead	wires
a hand drill and saw	screws
a light bulb in a holder	a bradawl
paints and paintbrush	a plank of wood
a small white ball	a large blue rubber ball

1 Paint a map of the world on the blue ball. With an adult's help, make a hole from pole to pole with a bradawl. Insert the straight wire.

2 Ask an adult to saw the wood into three strips. Glue them together to make a cross shape. Each arm will represent one of the seasons.

3 Screw the light bulb (the sun) to the center of the cross.

4 Make a hole in the white ball (the moon), and mount it on the bent wire, as shown below.

5 With an adult's help, drill a hole in each arm of the base for Earth's wire. Each hole must tilt by 23° to show how Earth's axis tilts. Use a protractor to guide the angle at which you drill. All four holes should tilt in the same direction.

6 Secure both Earth and moon wires in the bead with glue.

By placing Earth and moon in each arm, you can see how the seasons occur. Below right, you can see the Northern Hemisphere in winter, tilted away from the sun; on the left, it is tilted toward the sun and is in summer.

In December, because of Earth's tilt, the Southern Hemisphere gets more concentrated light and heat from the sun. It is summer in the south and winter in the north.

In March and September, both hemispheres receive the same amount of light. In the north, it is spring in March and autumn in September. In the south, the seasons are reversed.

On two days each year, around March 21 and September 23, there are 12 hours of daylight and 12 hours of darkness everywhere on Earth (except at the poles). These days are called the spring and autumn equinoxes. Using your model, can you explain why the equinoxes happen on these dates?

In June, Earth is halfway around its orbit – the Northern Hemisphere is tilted toward the sun and the Southern is tilted away, so it is summer in the north and winter in the south.

In December, the sun never rises in the Arctic Circle around the North Pole, and it is dark all day. But at the South Pole, the sun never sets, and it is light at midnight. Can you see why? How long are the days at the poles in June?

The equator is never tilted far from the direct rays of the sun. This is why the seasons hardly vary in countries lying along the equator. Days and nights are always about 12 hours long.

12 Solar Power

On a sunny day you can feel the heat coming off the ground, once the **energy** of the sun has heated it. The sun supplies enough energy to each square yard of Earth's surface to power several electric light bulbs. If we could trap just a fraction of this energy, we would no longer need to burn polluting fuels, such as coal and oil.

You will need

tape
cardboard
a large foil pie pan
two thermometers
a terra-cotta flowerpot

scissors
a bradawl
wooden dowel
a black squash ball

1 Make a hole in the center of the pie pan with the point of the scissors. Make a straight cut from the edge of the pan to the hole.

2 Overlap the cut edges so that the base of the pan curves like a satellite dish.

MAKE it WORK!

This simple **solar** heater uses a curved reflector to concentrate sunlight and heat the air inside a ball. Solar power stations in the United States and Israel use the same method. Large mirrors focus sunlight on water pipes or boilers. Steam from the boilers turns turbines to make electricity.

3 Ask an adult to make two holes in the squash ball at 90° to each other, with a bradawl. One hole is to mount the ball on the dowel, the other is for you to insert a thermometer.

4 Use cardboard and tape to fix the dish reflector at an angle on top of the flowerpot.

5 Push the dowel through the hole in the center of the pan. Mount the ball on top of the dowel. Place your solar heater in the sun. You may need to adjust the angle of the pan and the height of the ball until sunlight is reflected onto the ball.

*One solar power plant in Wisconsin has almost 10,000 reflectors. Each **solar panel** measures 3 ft x 6 ft, and together they produce enough energy to run a large factory.*

Now you are ready to test your solar heater. Use the thermometers to measure the temperature of the surrounding air and the temperature inside the ball. As Earth is constantly spinning, you will need to move the reflector dish to keep the sun focused on the ball. In real solar power stations, the mirrors are moved automatically by computer, so that they track the sun as it crosses the sky.

Black surfaces heat up more rapidly in the sun than white or silver ones. The silver surface of the pan reflects the light. The black surface of the ball absorbs the sun's energy. Make a note of the temperature reached inside the black ball. Then replace the black ball with a white Ping-Pong ball and repeat the experiment. Does the white ball get as hot?

Earth's nearest neighbor, the moon, is a barren, uninhabitable rock that orbits Earth. The moon can be dazzling, but it does not produce light itself. We can only see the moon because, like a mirror, it reflects light from the sun. The side of the moon facing the sun is brightly lit, but the side facing away from it is in dark shadow. The moon's appearance goes through a series of phases as it moves around Earth.

Use this simple model to see why the moon appears to change as it moves in its orbit.

You will need

a bradawl, wire	a flashlight
paint, cardboard	a rubber ball

1 Paint the ball with black, gray, and white paint to make a model moon, as below.

2 Ask an adult to help make a hole through the moon with a bradawl and mount it on the wire.

3 Fix the flashlight at eye level and darken the rest of the room. The flashlight is the sun.

New Moon

4 Hold the moon by the wire and face the flashlight with the moon between your head (Earth) and the flashlight (the sun). With the moon in this position you can only see the side in shadow. This is a new moon, as above left.

MAKE it WORK!

The moon takes 27½ days to orbit Earth. As the moon travels around Earth, we see different parts of its sunlit face. When the side of the moon facing us has no sunlight on it, it is invisible. This is the new moon. The phases of the moon repeat every 29½ days.

5 Now move the moon in a counterclockwise orbit. At first you see a bright crescent, then a half-lit moon. When the moon is halfway around its orbit you can look directly toward the brightly lit side. This is a full moon. As the moon continues its path, the changes reverse. Paint the moon's phases on a 30-day chart.

At times the moon appears brightly lit, and at other times it is shaded. But whatever its phase, the moon always shows the same face to Earth. The model above shows how the moon turns as it orbits, keeping one side hidden from view. The dark side of the moon has only been seen directly by the Apollo astronauts.

2 Ask an adult to help bend the wire and thread on the Earth and moon. Secure the model to a base with a lump of plasticine.

3 The moon orbits counterclockwise around Earth's equator. Mark the direction in which the moon travels with an arrow.

Full Moon

You will need

paints, cardboard, wire
a rubber ball, a bead
a small ball or marble

plasticine
a bradawl
a protractor

As you turn the moon around Earth, it turns with the wire, always showing the same face to Earth. The model above is not to scale. The moon should be 5 feet from Earth for the model to accurately reflect the real distance between the two.

1 Paint the model Earth and moon. Now cut a disk of cardboard and, using a protractor, mark every 13.3° on the disk to show the moon's motion each day. You should have 27 lines.

*The Moon is 250,000 mi from Earth and has a diameter of 2,160 mi, which means that it is approximately a quarter of the size of Earth. Because the phases of the moon repeat every 29½ days, we divide our years into 12 months. There is not an exact number of days in a **lunar** month, nor an exact number of lunar months in a year, so we have created months with 28, 29, 30, and 31 days. The full moon occurs at a different time each month.*

On July 20, 1969, Neil Armstrong became the first person to set foot on the moon. He traveled from Earth with Edwin Aldrin and Michael Collins. The astronauts were launched into space inside a capsule on top of Saturn V, one of the most powerful rockets ever built. Their mission was called Apollo 11.

MAKE it WORK!
Make a model of the Saturn V rocket (opposite). Look at the models on the right to see the different stages of the Apollo 11 mission.

You will need
glue	balsa wood
tape	a craft knife
wire	thin cardboard
a saw	Velcro patches
paints	cardboard tube
stickers	Earth and moon from p.14
scissors	thick and thin wooden dowel

1 Cut a 7-in.- and a 9-in.- length of cardboard tube **a** and **b**. Decorate as shown. Leave $^3/_8$ in. of **b** uncovered; cut a slit in it and fold the edges so that they overlap. Slot **b** into **a**.

2 Cut three cardboard stabilizer fins, **c**, glue in position, as shown far right. Cut and paint three short dowels, **d**. Glue them to the base of **a**.

3 Make a 3-in.-long cone, **e**. Cut a 3-in. piece of 1-in.-diameter dowel, **f**. Decorate as shown.

4 Cut a short dowel, **g**. Make two cardboard cones, **h** and **j**; glue to **g**, as shown in 10, right.

5 Glue four small Velcro patches to the top of **g**. Cut out four protective covers from thin cardboard, **i**, as shown. Tape the covers to the top of **f**.

6 For the lunar module, cut two balsa-wood shapes **k** and **l**. Glue them together as shown in 6, right. Attach four wires, **m**, to make legs. Place the module inside the protective cover **f** and **i**.

7 For the launch escape tower, **n**, ask an adult to shape a piece of thin dowel at both ends, using a craft knife. Paint it and glue it to **j**.

Stages of the Apollo 11 mission

1. Shortly after takeoff, the first stage of the Saturn V rocket fell away. The second stage carried Apollo higher before it, too, fell away.

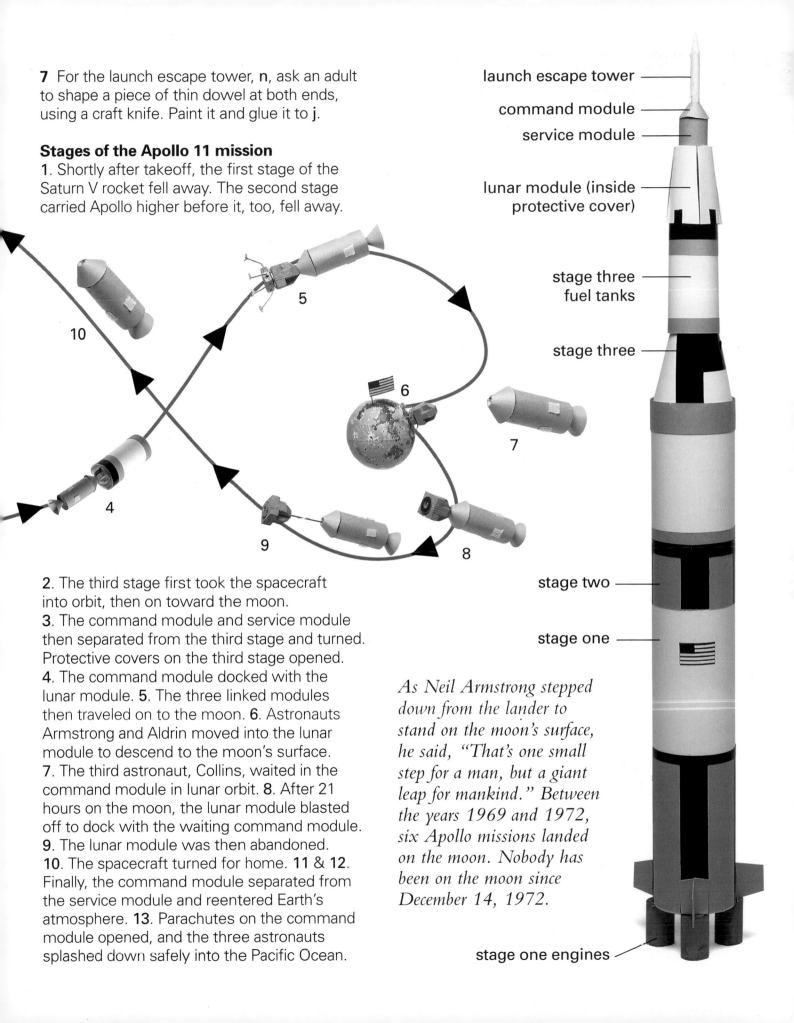

launch escape tower

command module

service module

lunar module (inside protective cover)

stage three fuel tanks

stage three

stage two

stage one

stage one engines

2. The third stage first took the spacecraft into orbit, then on toward the moon.
3. The command module and service module then separated from the third stage and turned. Protective covers on the third stage opened.
4. The command module docked with the lunar module. **5**. The three linked modules then traveled on to the moon. **6**. Astronauts Armstrong and Aldrin moved into the lunar module to descend to the moon's surface.
7. The third astronaut, Collins, waited in the command module in lunar orbit. **8**. After 21 hours on the moon, the lunar module blasted off to dock with the waiting command module.
9. The lunar module was then abandoned.
10. The spacecraft turned for home. **11 & 12**. Finally, the command module separated from the service module and reentered Earth's atmosphere. **13**. Parachutes on the command module opened, and the three astronauts splashed down safely into the Pacific Ocean.

As Neil Armstrong stepped down from the lander to stand on the moon's surface, he said, "That's one small step for a man, but a giant leap for mankind." Between the years 1969 and 1972, six Apollo missions landed on the moon. Nobody has been on the moon since December 14, 1972.

Eclipses are the biggest shadows you will ever see. A solar eclipse occurs when the moon passes between the sun and Earth, casting its shadow on Earth. In a lunar eclipse, Earth's shadow covers the moon. The moon's shadow is smaller than Earth, so a solar eclipse can only be seen where the shadow falls. But a lunar eclipse can be seen from anywhere on Earth that is facing the moon.

MAKE it WORK!
Use the model you made on page 6 to see how eclipses of the sun and moon happen.

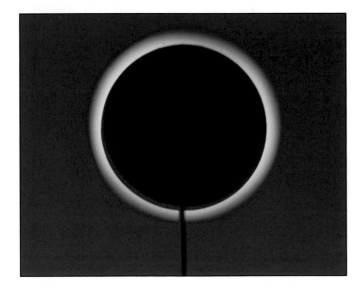

Although the sun is 400 times bigger than the moon, it is also 400 times farther away. This is why they appear to be almost the same size.

This is how the sun, Earth, and moon line up in a lunar eclipse, which can happen twice a year.

This is how the sun, moon, and Earth are lined up during a solar eclipse. The moon blocks out the sun's light almost completely.

Earth lies between the sun and the moon, casting a dark shadow on the moon.

People on the night side of Earth see the moon vanish into shadow for an hour or more.

As the moon moves in its orbit, it comes between Earth and the sun. The moon casts a shadow over Earth's surface.

The eclipse is only total at the center of the shadow. The longest time a total eclipse can last is just under eight minutes.

The first person to look at the stars and planets with a telescope is thought to be the great Italian scientist Galileo, nearly 400 years ago. Using a simple telescope, very like the one shown on this page, he drew sketches of the mountains on the moon and discovered that Jupiter has moons and that the **Milky Way** is a countless mass of stars.

You will need
cardboard tubes
two lenses
scissors
tape

1 You will need to experiment to find out how long the telescope tube must be. Stand by a window and hold one lens at arm's length. Hold another lens to one eye. Slowly bring the first lens toward the second until you can see a clear image of the scene outside through both lenses (the image will be upside down). Try different lens pairs to find the best combination.

MAKE it WORK!
Construct a simple astronomical telescope with two magnifying lenses. Lenses are curved disks of glass. The lens through which the light enters the telescope is the **objective** lens. The second lens is the **eyepiece**.

2 Cut a piece of tube about an inch longer than the distance needed between the lenses. Cut this tube in half. Make a slit along the length of one of the tubes. Overlap the edges slightly, so that it slides inside the other tube.

3 Fix the lenses to either end of the telescope tube using tape, as shown. Cut out a circle of card for the eyepiece and tape in place.

To study the moon through your telescope, slide the tubes in and out to **focus** the image sharply.

BE CAREFUL! Never look at the sun through a telescope, binoculars, or with your naked eye. You could be blinded.

Using your solarscope you can study sunspots. These are cooler areas on the sun's surface. They move slowly from east to west because the sun is spinning.

A safe way to study the sun is to use a solarscope. Cut a hole in a large sheet of cardboard so that it just fits over one lens of a pair of binoculars. Put the binoculars on a pole and point them at the sun. **Do not look through the binoculars!** Cast an image of the sun on a piece of white cardboard behind the eyepiece.

Modern astronomers use telescopes with huge mirrors instead of objective lenses. These are often used in observatories on remote mountaintop sites where the air is clear. Space telescopes view the planets from above Earth's atmosphere. The Hubble Space Telescope was launched in 1990 and has a main mirror 8 ft across.

22 Orbits and Gravity

Orbits are the circular or **elliptical** courses that planets and satellites follow, repeating their motion over and over again. There is always a massive object at the center of a planet's or moon's orbit. The sun is at the center of Earth's orbit and Earth is at the center of the moon's orbit. It is the force of **gravity** between the objects that keeps the orbit going – like the pull on a weighted string when you whirl it in a circle.

MAKE it WORK!
Try drawing orbits. Some orbits are circles. Others are stretched circles called ellipses.

To draw an ellipse you will need

pencils	paper
drawing pins	string
a drawing board	

1 Pin a sheet of paper to the board.

2 Tie a loop of string and fix it to the board with two drawing pins about 3 in. apart.

3 Stretch the loop with a pencil. Draw an ellipse by moving the pencil around the pins, keeping the string taut.

Experiment with the spacing of the pins and the length of the loop to draw different shaped ellipses. The two pins are at points called the **foci** of the ellipse. In our solar system, the sun sits at one focus of each planet's elliptical orbit.

Studying orbits

The planets farthest from the sun travel more slowly in their orbits than those that are nearby. This model shows how an orbit speeds up as it gets smaller.

1 Ask an adult to help you drill a hole in the block just big enough for the dowel. Fix the dowel firmly in place.

2 Tie one end of the string to the top of the pole. Tape the other end to the ball. Launch the ball into orbit around the pole.

What happens to the ball's speed as the string winds around the pole and the orbit gets smaller?

Into orbit

A satellite must be launched at the right speed and angle if it is to stay in orbit around Earth. If it goes too fast, it will escape from Earth's gravity and disappear into space. Too slow, and it will spiral back into the atmosphere and burn up.

You will need

a rubber ball
a wooden block
wooden dowel

tape
string
a hand drill

The first man in space, Yuri Gagarin, took just 80 minutes to orbit Earth in 1961. This is the orbital time, or period, for any satellite just above Earth's atmosphere. Television satellites take 24 hours to orbit Earth. These satellites keep step with Earth's rotation, so that they are always over the same place on Earth.

The sun is at the center of our solar system. Orbiting the sun are nine planets, their moons, and millions of smaller objects such as asteroids and comets. From the sun out, the planets are Mercury, Venus, Earth, Mars, Jupiter, Saturn, Uranus, Neptune, and Pluto. Each planet moves at a different speed in its orbit. The inner planets travel much faster than the more distant planets.

MAKE it WORK!
Move the planets around this model solar system calendar to compare how long it takes them to orbit the sun.

The stickers on each orbit, up to and including Saturn, represent one month. After Saturn, they represent one year.

You will need

adhesive paper rings	cardboard
rubber or plastic balls	scissors
a drawing compass, wire	glue, paints
a large sheet of black cardboard	a bradawl
a flashlight or low-wattage lamp	scissors

1 Paint the balls to make the nine planets, as shown above. Ask an adult to help you make holes through the balls and fix them onto the wires. The sun is made with half a plastic ball, fixed over a low-wattage lamp or flashlight.

► The model right shows the position of the planets in March; far right: the positions of the planets in June.

2 Cut an elliptical shape from the cardboard; cut a large circle from the center. Draw eight orbits on the circle. Glue the circle in the ellipse.

3 Stick 12 equally spaced markers along Earth's orbit (third from the sun). Paint them a different color for each month.

4 Place the markers for the other planets as shown. All the planets are in line with January. The planets orbit at different speeds, so distances between the markers along each orbit willl vary. To calculate the distance (in degrees) traveled by each planet in a month, divide 360° by the number of months each planet takes to orbit the sun (see chart).

Orbital times in Earth months:

Mercury	*3*
Venus	*7*
Earth	*12*
Mars	*23*
Jupiter	*142*
Saturn	*354*
Uranus	*1008*
Neptune	*1978*
Pluto	*2976*

Pluto travels in an elliptical orbit. One rotation takes 249 years.

What's inside a planet? If you sliced Earth in half, you would find it has a hot, metal core of mainly nickel and iron. Surrounding this core are layers of rock and other metals. We live on Earth's outer crust, a thin layer of rock which is between four and 24 miles thick.

3 With an adult's help, use a craft knife to cut slots (as shown below right) in each pair of planet disks. Fold the sections of the disk and slide them together to assemble your planets. Then mount your planets on the wires, securing them with tape.

What are the planets like?
Mercury has a surface temperature hot enough to melt lead. It is thought to have a metal core surrounded by thin layers of rock.

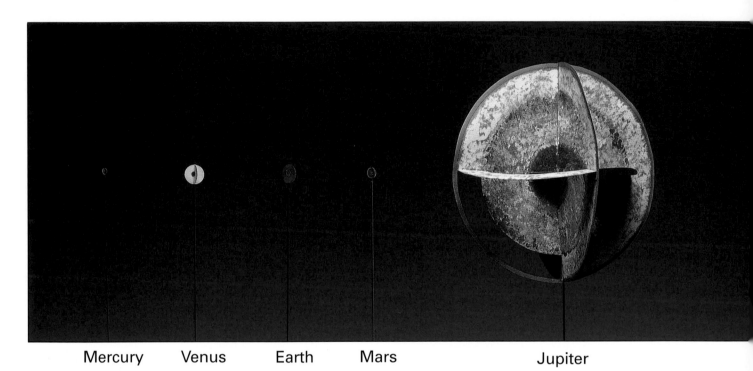

| Mercury | Venus | Earth | Mars | Jupiter |

MAKE it WORK!
These models of the planets show what scientists think they look like on the inside.

You will need
tape	scissors
paints	a craft knife
wire and cardboard	a drawing compass

1 Each planet is made from two identical cardboard disks. Use the compass to draw circles to the scale of the planets (see table opposite).

2 Draw rings to show the different layers within each planet and paint them different colors.

Venus is almost the same size as Earth and probably has a similar core surrounded by layers of rock. Venus has a dense atmosphere, but this is nothing like Earth's. It is filled with acid droplets and is as hot as the surface of Mercury.

Earth is the watery planet. Water covers more than two-thirds of Earth's surface. The surface temperature (27°C) is just right for life, and it is the only planet on which life is known.

Mars, the red planet, is about half the diameter of Earth. It has a small iron core surrounded by rocky layers. It has a very thin atmosphere and is much colder than Earth.

Jupiter is the largest planet. Unlike the four inner planets (Mercury, Venus, Earth, and Mars), it is not solid. It has a solid rock core, surrounded by a very dense atmosphere of cold, swirling gas. A spacecraft could not land on Jupiter – it would just sink into the gas.

Jupiter has a huge, swirling weather system the size of the planet Earth on its surface, called the Great Red Spot. Scientists are still not sure how Jupiter was formed.

Saturn, Neptune, and Uranus are all "gas giants" like Jupiter. Saturn has spectacular rings made from millions of tiny rocks orbiting like moons. Draw the rings on a cardboard disk and attach them with wires to your Saturn model.

Pluto is the smallest of all the planets and the most distant from the sun. It has never been explored, but is believed to be made up of a rocky core surrounded by layers of ice and frozen gas. Pluto's moon is called Charon.

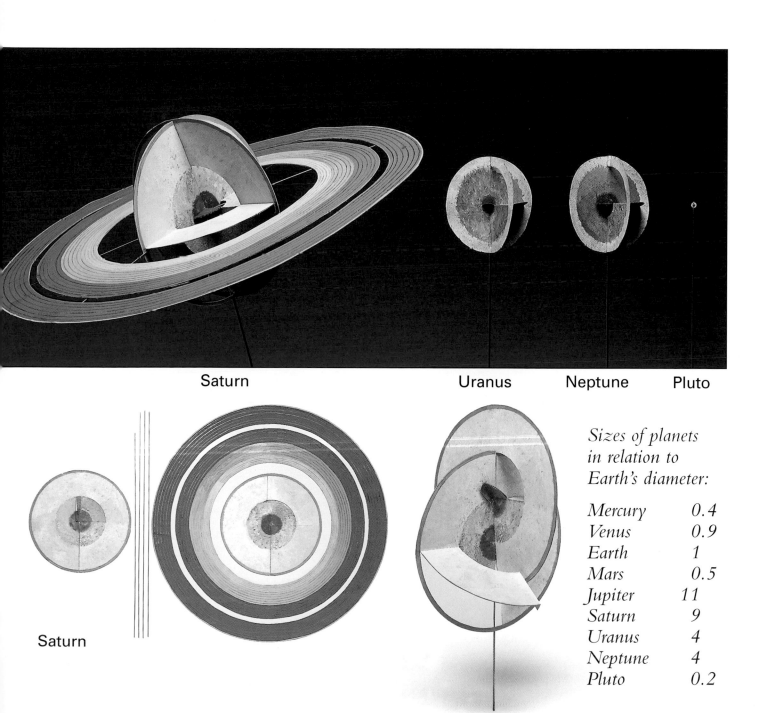

Saturn   Uranus   Neptune   Pluto

Saturn

Sizes of planets in relation to Earth's diameter:

Mercury	*0.4*
Venus	*0.9*
Earth	*1*
Mars	*0.5*
Jupiter	*11*
Saturn	*9*
Uranus	*4*
Neptune	*4*
Pluto	*0.2*

28 Meteoroids and Comets

Meteoroids are pieces of rock often left behind by **comets**. As meteoroids enter Earth's atmosphere, friction makes them burn up and they become shooting stars. The moon has no atmosphere to protect it from collisions. It is covered with craters made by meteorites hitting its surface.

You will need
newspapers
flour or damp sand
a large tray or oven dish
ball bearings or marbles

1 Protect the work surface with newspaper. Fill the tray with flour or damp sand. Drop the meteors into the tray to make model craters.

Experiment to see how the size of the meteor and the height from which you drop it affects the crater.

A meteoroid that enters the atmosphere is called a **meteor**. If it lands without burning up, it is called a meteorite.

MAKE it WORK!
The surface of the moon is pitted with craters. Make your own moon surface and see how craters are formed. There are meteorite craters on Earth, too. The Barringer meteorite landed in Arizona, leaving a crater almost a mile wide.

Comets are balls of rock, ice, and frozen gas that orbit the sun in very elliptical paths. As comets get close to the sun, some of the gas boils off, making the comet look as if it has a tail, and pieces of rock come away. These rock fragments become meteoroids. Halley's comet comes close to Earth every 76 years. Last seen in 1986, it is due to reappear in 2062.

Asteroids are potato-shaped lumps of rock left over from the time when the planets formed. Most asteroids travel in a belt between the orbits of Mars and Jupiter. With some cardboard and paint, you can add the asteroid belts to your solar system model.

The **Trojans** are two groups of asteroids that follow the same orbit as Jupiter around the sun. Make and paint two cardboard asteroid groups like those shown below for the Trojans. Place them in Jupiter's orbit on your model.

Saturn

Mercury

Venus

Jupiter

Mars

Trojan asteroid

Trojan asteroid

ranus

Earth

main asteroid belt

Neptune

a: irregular asteroid
b: white asteroid
c: black asteroid

a

b

c

Some scientists think that asteroids would make good "stepping stones" for the **colonization** of space (see p 30-31). Space stations could be set up on larger asteroids. They could also be mined for raw materials.

There are millions of asteroids orbiting the asteroid belts. They range in size from grains of sand to lumps bigger than Mt. Everest. The biggest, called Ceres, is 567 mi in diameter.

Imagine climbing aboard a spacecraft and setting out to explore the solar system, perhaps stopping to visit a colony on Mars and going on to see the asteroids. There are plans for a trip to Mars within your lifetime. So far, the farthest space journey made by humans has been to the moon. However, unmanned robot probes have landed on, or flown by, every planet except Pluto.

You will need

tape and glue	wire
a Ping-Pong ball	beads
a battery and wires	scissors
a bulb and bulb holder	cardboard
polystyrene packing foam	a craft knife
fishing wire or wooden dowel	a plastic ball
a transparent colored plastic tube	

1 Use a plastic ball cut in half for the probe's body, **e**. Make a hole big enough for the bulb to go through and two holes for the bulb wires. To make the beacon, **f**, follow steps **a** to **d** below. Tape the battery inside the probe's body.

i

h

e

f

k

g

l

MAKE it WORK!

Make your own space probe based on the Voyager probes. These probes are known as fly-by probes, because their **sensors** record information as they pass close to the planets.

2 To make the probe dish, **g**, cut out a circle of cardboard 12 in. in diameter. Cut a segment out of it, as above. Overlap the cut edges and tape or glue them together. The dish points to Earth to transmit and receive radio signals.

a

b

c

d

3 Make the probe platform, **h**, by cutting out a circle with a 6-in. diameter. Make 12 cuts, ³/₈ in. deep, around the circle, then bend and glue into shape. Glue the platform to the probe body, as shown below.

4 For the atmosphere probe, **i**, glue half a Ping-Pong ball to the back of the platform. For the camera, stick a tube of black cardboard onto a wire and tape it to the body. For the antennae, **k**, glue beads to straight wires and attach as shown.

7 Either suspend your fly-by probe from a hook on fishing wire, or tape it to a wooden dowel glued to a base board, as shown below.

The Voyager 2 probe was launched in 1977. Since then it has flown by Jupiter (1979), Saturn (1981), Uranus (1986), and Neptune (1989). Voyager has transmitted thousands of pictures back to Earth, enabling scientists to make many new discoveries.

5 For the boom, **l**, ask an adult to help you cut and fold a piece of black cardboard into a triangular shape as shown left. Glue the boom to the dish.

6 Make asteroids with painted pieces of polystyrene foam stuck on to lengths of wire.

Two Viking probes landed on Mars in 1976. They sent back 3,000 photographic images, took soil samples that were examined in a specially built laboratory, and measured the temperature and wind speed on the surface. No recognizable signs of life were found.

Complete your planetarium

Now you can complete the model planetarium that you started to make on page 37. Once all the stars have been punched with holes and joined to make constellations, you will need to glue all the cardboard segments together. Make sure that you glue them in the correct order to make the Northern and Southern Hemispheres.

Northern Hemisphere

4 To make a star dome or a globe that you can view from the outside, lay the segments in order with the star patterns facing out.

Southern Hemisphere

5 Now fold and glue the segments together to make north and south celestial hemispheres. Make sure the segments are in order.

6 To view the stars, stand the hemispheres over a flashlight or a low-wattage lamp and turn off the lights in the room. The stars will shine just as they do on a clear night.

Although the stars are constantly moving, they are so distant they appear fixed. Because of this, we can map them on a celestial sphere.

If you lived at the North Pole you would be able to see all the stars in the northern celestial hemisphere when it is dark. At the South Pole you would have a clear view of all the southern stars.

People who live between the equator and the North Pole or the South Pole see different stars at different times of the year. This is because Earth is orbiting the sun and the dark side of Earth faces in a slightly different direction each night.

North of the equator, in the United States for example, you see all the northern stars and some of the southern ones during the year. South of the equator, in Australia or New Zealand for example, all of the southern stars and some of the northern ones are visible. However, if you live on the equator, during the course of a year it is possible to see the complete celestial sphere.

Polaris, the Pole Star, lies almost directly above the North Pole. If you find Polaris you can work out which way you are facing and will never lose your direction on a starry night.

The red line on the model is called the plane of the ecliptic. This is the path that the sun seems to take through the stars during the year.

If you want to see the stars in your model in exactly the same way that you would view them in a planetarium, then you have to be able to look up into it. In this case, you will need to glue the segments together with the star patterns facing inward. If you do not put it together in this way, the patterns will look back to front.

If you watch the stars during the course of a night, they seem to move in the sky, turning around Polaris, the Pole Star, in the north. But really the stars are fixed and it is Earth that is spinning. Try turning your model planetarium above your head; then keep the planetarium still and turn your head instead. Both actions make the stars appear to move.

Have you ever studied the clouds and thought you could see faces or animals? Stars make shapes in the sky in just the same way. In our mind's eye we can draw lines between the stars and join them to make patterns called constellations. The ancient Greeks created legends about the figures they saw in the stars. They gave the constellations names, such as Orion the hunter, Taurus the bull, and Aquarius the water gatherer.

MAKE it WORK!
This model shows how stars in the Big Dipper (which is part of the Ursa Major, or Great Bear, constellation) are arranged in three dimensions. The stars only make the pattern we see when they are viewed from one particular direction.

You will need
wires
a glue gun
a hand drill
yellow paint
wooden dowel
dark blue cardboard
a base board (8 in. x 12 in.)
seven bulbs and seven holders

scissors
a battery
insulated wire

1 Cut out a piece of cardboard that will overlap your base board by 2 in. Cover base board with the cardboard, sticking it down with glue. Mark out and rule the cardboard with a $3/4$-in. square grid, as shown below. The squares represent light-years (the distance traveled by light in a year).

2 Using the grid as your guide, ask an adult to help you drill seven holes big enough for the dowel posts.

3 Cut seven lengths of doweling, as shown below left, and glue them into the holes.

4 Glue the bulb holders onto the top of the posts and screw in the bulbs.

5 Wire the bulbs as shown above and connect the battery.

Alkaid   Mizar   Alioth   Megrez   Phekda   Merak   Dubhe

It's best to view your constellation from a distance in a dark room, or outside on a dark night.

The Big Dipper, or Plow, is part of the Ursa Major constellation. It is one of the easiest star patterns to find in the northern sky. The stars on the right, Merak and Dubhe, point up to Polaris.

250
225
200
175
150
125
100
75
50

Walk around the model to see how the shape of the Plow changes from different viewpoints.

Astronomers use 88 named constellations to find their way around the night sky.

As Earth spins, the stars seem to move in the sky. Earth's night side faces in different directions at different times of year, so some stars that can be seen in winter are not visible in summer.

Canis major
Leo
Ursa major
Virgo
Libra
Hercules
Sagittarius
Cetus
Pegasus
Aquarius
Capricornus

Finding constellations in the night sky can be difficult. A planisphere is a special chart that shows where constellations are at different times of the year.

MAKE it WORK!

You can make a model star finder to show you how a planisphere works. If you want an accurate planisphere, you must buy one specially made for the **latitude** where you live. The star finder shown on this page works for northern Europe and the northern parts of North America.

You will need

cardboard	glue
scissors	a star chart
luminous paints	a paper fastener
a magnetic compass	

1 Cut out two circles from cardboard: one should be about an inch smaller in diameter than the other.

2 Copy the stars that are visible from the Northern Hemisphere from your star map. Glue the photocopy onto the larger disk, as shown below left. Draw over the constellations with luminous paint.

3 Make 12 equally spaced marks around the large disk to represent the months. Using your paints, number the months from 1 to 12 and then divide each into four and mark each quarter, as shown above left.

4 Cut a window from small disk, as shown above. Leave a "finger" of cardboard reaching to the center.

5 Mark the hours, from 8 P.M. to 4 A.M., on the edge of the small disk. The space between each hour should be half the space given to each month on the big disk. Mark north with an N and an arrow, at 12 midnight, as above.

6 Make a hole in the center of both disks and join them together with the paper fastener.

To use the star finder, turn the upper disk to line up the time with the month. Now, use a compass to find magnetic North and turn to face it, holding your star finder in front of you. You should be able to see the stars shown in the window when you look at the night sky.

▲ The night sky at midnight, January 1

Try to view the night sky in an area where there are no street lights; otherwise you will only be able to see the brightest stars.

If you buy a planisphere for a different latitude, the window will be in a different position on the upper disk.

With your naked eye you can see about 3,000 stars, but with a pair of binoculars you can see many more. All the individual stars we can see are part of a huge "star city," or galaxy, called the Milky Way. There may be as many as 100 billion stars in the Milky Way, but it is not the only galaxy in the universe. There are billions of galaxies, each made from gas, dust, and billions of stars.

Galaxies are made up of billions of stars, many of which are like our sun. Most are so far away that they can only be seen with the use of a powerful telescope. The light from the farthest galaxies takes millions of years to reach Earth. Our galaxy is the Milky Way, which is thought to contain around 100 billion stars. It has spiral arms like the model below. Our sun lives in one of the arms.

an elliptical galaxy

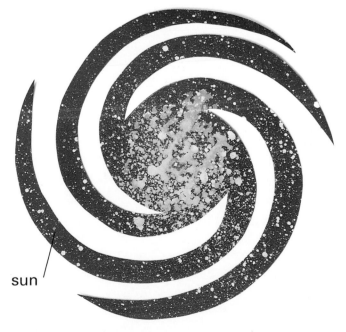

sun

The Milky Way (spiral galaxy)

Throughout history, people have asked many questions about the universe. One of the great puzzles was "Does the universe have an edge or does it go on forever?" The great scientist Albert Einstein thought that space need not have an edge because it may be curved.

When a star dies, gravity makes it collapse. If the star was a giant, it could form a black hole.

MAKE it WORK!

The models here will help you understand two key ideas about the universe: the way a massive star curves the space around it, and how expansion makes galaxies move apart.

2 Cut a strip of cardboard, 1 yd. long x 3 in. wide. Curl it into a ring and tape the ends, as shown below. Stretch the rubber over the ring and secure it with tape.

To see how a black hole works you will need

rubber sheeting
strong cardboard
a drawing compass
a heavy ball bearing or marble

strong tape
a felt-tip pen
a protractor
scissors

3 Drop the ball bearing or marble into the center of your universe.

1 Cut a 36-in.-diameter circle of rubber. Draw circles on it 2 in. apart. Use a protractor to measure diagonal lines across every 20°.

When the rubber sheet is flat the lines on the grid are evenly spaced. This shows what space is like when it is empty. When you add the ball bearing the grid stretches – you can see how the universe curves around a massive star. A curved universe need not have an edge, just as the surface of a football has no edge.

When astronomers look at distant galaxies, they can see them moving away from us. This shows that the universe is getting bigger all the time. It now seems that the universe was formed by a huge explosion, called the big bang, 15 billion years ago. Ever since then, space has continued to expand.

Every galaxy on the balloon moves away from every other galaxy. This is exactly what is happening in space as the universe expands. The galaxies remain the same size, but get farther apart from one another.

On your model universe, notice how more distant galaxies move farther apart, each time you blow air into the balloon, than galaxies that are neighbors. This is just what astronomers see when they look into space through powerful telescopes. The farther a galaxy is from the Milky Way (our galaxy), the faster it is moving away.

To make an expanding universe you will need
a ruler
balloons
felt-tip pens

1 Using a felt-tip pen, draw galaxies all over a flat balloon, as shown at the top of the page.

2 Blow up the balloon, a little at a time. As you blow it up, the distance between the galaxies grows larger. Measure these distances.

Astronomers think that the expansion of the universe is slowing down. Perhaps one day it will stop completely and will start to collapse again. This would be similar to a balloon shrinking when you let air out of it. If this does happen, everything in the universe will collapse and it will end with what scientists call the "big crunch!" But don't worry, the "big crunch" is not expected to happen for billions of years.

Asteroid Asteroids are rocks that range in size from a diameter of one mile to a few hundred miles. Most of them orbit the sun in the asteroid belt that lies between the orbits of Jupiter and Mars.

Axis An axis is an imaginary line around which something turns. Earth spins around an axis running between the North and South poles.

Black holes These are holes in space where gravity is so strong that nothing, not even light, can escape once it has fallen in. They form when massive stars burn out and gravity crushes together the matter left over.

Calibrate This term refers to making or to checking marks on a measuring scale, such as a ruler or a sundial.

Celestial This means anything to do with the sky. When we look at the stars in the sky, we imagine that the stars are fixed to a revolving celestial sphere.

Colonize When a group of people move to a new country or planet and settle there, this is called colonizing.

Comet A ball of rock, ice, and frozen gas that orbits the sun. When a comet comes near the sun, parts melt and boil off to form the comet's tail.

Compass (magnetic) This is an instrument with a magnetized needle that always points at the North Pole. It is used for direction finding.

Compass (drawing) This instrument is used to draw circles. It has two hinged legs: one leg acts as a fixed point, the other holds a pencil or a pen.

Eclipse An eclipse happens when the sun's light is blocked by Earth or the moon. A lunar eclipse occurs when Earth blocks the light between the sun and the moon.

Ellipse An ellipse is a special curved shape, which looks like a flattened or stretched circle. The orbits that some of the planets make around the sun are elliptical.

Energy When something has energy it can make things move, change, or warm up.

Equator The equator is an imaginary line around Earth halfway between the poles that divide the Northern and Southern hemispheres.

Eyepiece The eyepiece of a telescope is the lens placed nearest the eye.

Foci (Plural of focus.) An ellipse has two foci. These are two special points, like the center of a circle around which the ellipse is drawn. The sun sits at one focus of Earth's elliptical orbit.

Focus To focus means to concentrate light to make a clear picture. Telescopes collect and focus the light from planets and stars. The focus of a lens is the point at which the light from a distant object, such as a star, is concentrated when it passes through the lens.

Galaxy A group of billions of stars in space.

Gnomon The pointer that casts a shadow on a sundial.

Gravity The force that makes things feel heavy and pulls them toward the ground. The force of gravity keeps the moon orbiting Earth and the planets orbiting the sun.

Hemisphere Half a sphere, like a dome. Earth is divided into two hemispheres – Northern and Southern.

Latitude The distance measured widthwise from the equator. The equator is 0°, while the North and South poles are at 90° latitude.

Lens A curved piece of glass or plastic, specially shaped to focus light.

Lunar Lunar refers to the moon; for example, the lunar surface.

Magnitude Another word for the brightness of a star, as seen from Earth.

Meteor The name given to a small piece of rock from space (a meteoroid) that has burned up on entering Earth's atmosphere.

Meteoroid A piece of rock or debris in space, often broken off from a comet.

Milky Way The Milky Way is our galaxy. The sun is just one of a billion stars that make up the Milky Way.

Nuclear reaction A change that happens when tiny particles from the center of atoms knock into each other. Nuclear reactions in stars give out the great amounts of energy that make stars shine.

Objective The objective lens of a telescope is the large lens that collects and focuses light from the stars.

Orbit The curved path followed by a planet, a moon, or a satellite as it spins around a more massive body.

Photosynthesis The process by which the green leaves on plants trap the energy of sunlight and use it to make food.

Sensors These are the thermometers, cameras, and other measuring instruments on probes and satellites. They are used to record information about a planet.

Solar Solar refers to the sun. For instance, in a solar eclipse, it is the sun's light that is blocked by the moon.

Solar panel A special panel that absorbs the sun's energy and converts it into electricity.

Space probes There are two types: fly-by probes and landers. A fly-by probe is an unmanned spacecraft sent to fly close by the planets. Its purpose is to gather information, collect samples, and record pictures to beam back to Earth. A lander has the same function as a fly-by, but it lands on a planet's surface.

Trojans Two groups of asteroids that follow the same orbit as Jupiter around the sun. They travel in front of, and behind, Jupiter.